MOHILAK

MOHILAK

Keana Aguila Labra

Fahmidan & Co. Publishing
Arlington, VA, USA / Kuwait City, Kuwait

<u>Land Acknowledgement in Support of Land Back Movement</u>

This book was written on Ohlone Tamyen land in the so-called "United States of America." In remembering the history of my family's history and immigration, we must also remember the legacies of colonialism that we benefit from and continue to benefit from today as settler-colonialists.

From Palestine to the Philippines, we are not free until all of us are free.

Fahmidan & Co. Publishing
Arlington, VA, USA / Kuwait City, Kuwait
© 2021 Fahmidan & Co. Publishing
© 2021 Keana Aguila Labra
All rights reserved.
First Digital Edition, September 2021
Author: Keana Aguila Labra
Illustrator: Farah Hasan
Design & Formatting: A.R. Salandy, Ranna K. Kisswani
Press Editors: Yasmine Dashti, Areeba Bhajikhara, Farah Hasan
www.fahmidan.net/
fahmidanpublishing@gmail.com

Para sa paborito kong tita,
the most travelled auntie:
Auntie Sugar,
she who taught me that dreams
are worth chasing

Contents

Happy Mother's Day   11

I. BIYAAN
    When Something More than Your Hometown is Lost   16
    To the Pianist who Refused to Play 'Work' by Rihanna
    for my Manghod's 21st Birthday   17
    Misalign   18
    Paksiw   19
    Sustained   20
    First   21
    The things I didn't know I loved   22
    Prayer for Opposites   24
    In which I learn from Rupi Kaur and say what I mean   26

II. LUHA
    They say every person contains a Universe, so I am one too   30
    An Ode to (Toxic) Masculinity   32
    Portrait of Josefa as Lola   34

III. HILAK
    How will you begin?   39
    November 19, 2020 at 3:50pm   40
    Asa ang Tanan?   42
    Dalaga   44
    The Effects of Trauma on Impressionable Adolescents
    is what it should have read   46
    When my future apo ask how their Lolo and I stayed

in love during the pandemic   48
Write a List of Your Achievements, what has lead
you to achieve them?   49
Multitudes   50
Personhood   51

IV.   KUSGAN
      Lineage   54

Acknowledgements   57
Portrait of a Bio as a Poem   63

Poetry shouldn't only be a confession
I want it to be more than that.

Romalyn Ante

Happy Mother's Day

i. I wish I were enough
but I was born in the transition
when the cold chokes the fall

all I've ever asked for
were her hands,

but today is her day.

ii. she and I exist in the transactional
yet I remain in the exchange.

MOHILAK

*The trouble is
some of us are
terribly tender.*

Upile Chisala

I.
BIYAAN

When Something More than Your Hometown is Lost

What was once
on the back of my hand
is replaced by doubt-

Is this where I turn
Is this where we kissed
Is this where our hearts broke?

To the Pianist who Refused to Play 'Work' by Rihanna for my Manghod's 21st Birthday
for Jamie Leanne Aguila Labra

After beignets,
after jazz,

after dueling pianos of a bygone era
when we believed we as a whole
would sacrifice for the greater good.

Smiling under lights of
green beads, bulbs, and cups
where I greeted a river god

for the first time, I
an ocean child
making wishes for more
under the sagittarius moon.

But for now,
we hold hands with
French tourists who tell us
we are so beautiful,
and we lay our skin bare
to the country road.

Misalign

Malignant growths are unmanageable,
it cracks below the surface
and my hands spiral out of control,

we'll fill in the flaws with silence.

My eyes steer without consideration.
I learn difficult truths
hoping to grow thicker skin,
(I flake under pressure.)

I do not benefit
out of this exchange

yet I linger,
yet I stay.

Paksiw is not solely the name of the food, it is a technique. To paksiw is to cook and simmer in vinegar. There is a paksiw for every Nanay, Tita, Ate, and Lola who ever cooked. For my Nay, it is paksiw na lechon. She grazes knives together, second nature, second daughter. Imagine her, sleepless and irritated, as my grandparents wake her and her siblings for the rush after Simbang Gabi. Eyelids closed and mind elsewhere. Fingers rolling embutido. Tradition creates muscle memory. And so my mother takes out her frustration on these knives, the anak ni mga magkakarne, Baby and Eddie of Baby and Eddie's meat shop in Tondo. This is probably why my mother hardly cooks, trauma seeping its way into acts we thought necessary. But on rare occasions, she wields her knives and laughs at the pig's head and feeds us paksiw na lechon. And it's as if I'm transported back in time, to my Lola and Lolo with black hair, taut skin, and smiles. I imagine my mother smiling too, paksiw poking out between pearly teeth.

Sustained

There is something about the northern air
the way the cold settles across my shoulders
I welcome its embrace
my steps meet the ground
my neck cranes upward
once I return to the shelter
of my dwelling
this calm will dissipate
so I breathe in the peace
I wish to carry inside

this quiet
reminds me of home.

First

My hands were turned upward,
eager to soothe the hard lines
of my mother's eyes
to seek acceptance is to seek ruin

Each confession that replayed
led to the prying of a carcass,

The flowers bloomed only
wishing to drink from the sun
but the leaves were
left with no room to grow.

But 'mothers' are not only found not in
the root of the word, but in the
exchanging of hands,

though she may not cradle
Me in the unconditional,
I have forged my own.

The things I didn't know I loved

We are asked to imagine anew.
I think of my lola and her garden.

This plant is "nakalimutan ko pala,"
a leaf for each of the three marias:
Josefa, Virginia, and Fe

edible and unlike its name,
it restores skin across her fingers.

It reminds me
the stretch of her perfume,
and her recipe for kangkong.

It journeys past her to
Luis Flores y Perez,
Katipunan,
lolo of my lola,
and he teaches me
to stake claim for myself.

Masucol means
to fight, and I imagine
his smile a wreath of flowers.

I eat another leaf from this plant
and the lola of my lola,
unnamed, stitches

words for me before
returning to the
sun on her cloth.

There is only one
of its kind, this
"nakalimutan ko pala,"

and I save the last leaf for my lola Josie
until I can find the plant for immortality.

Prayer for Opposites
After 'Long Live the Tribe of Fatherless Girls'

we are the lost days and fist
in burning abysses, forced to provide for
a family at the start of youth, but we
do not ask for the pulsating limbs and
insatiable appetites, we are scarred with
our need to want and our need to love.

I will always be at the disadvantage,
because in my eyes, you are infallible

There is nothing I can change nor
can I escape, trapped in my own cage
that I must remain in this state
because in my eyes, you are infallible

and no matter what object morphs the
bones in my face and reddens the pink
upon my cheek, we will always love and
we will love unconditionally and with
forgiveness, prostrating ourselves into

grovelling earth, there is no record of a
father ever returning whole. amen.

In which I learn from Rupi Kaur and say what I mean

I wish time
stayed in my pocket.
In between my fingers.
But, it prefers the
tip of my nose:
always in sight
but slightly out
of focus.

What we speak
always returns.
Joy Harjo

II.
LUHA

Lola can't sleep without milk. Lolo can't sleep at all. I crush one then two Benadryls and contemplate a third. I crush a third. I stir the pink-white powder into Sleepytime tea and mix until there is only green and then I pray. And then I am let down every two hours except on nights Lola takes pity on me. The dark circles under our eyes confusing others who thought us younger than our actual age. She calls my brother over to do yard work and sweep leaves and hack at trees. She shows us the ones she did herself proud of her handiwork and independence while we beg her next time to let one of us know so we can do it instead. Now that Lolo is gone, she does not lift a finger. Portrait of ghost as warning. Of inevitability. She does not see us. The space she kept for understanding disappears and we meet spokes when we expect feather down. I leave in my own tea leaves until it becomes dark and murky because I envision an entirely different future. One where I am defined as caretaking in a more severe way. Lola can't sleep without milk. But now I know there will come a day with only memory.

They say every person contains a Universe, so I am one too

My stars a voice,
a voice as salve,
a voice as constant.

A voice as
contours of my chest
from the sound of my exhale,
the tilt in my tone.

The sun the sum of my lolas,
and we share a cup of coffee
whenever I successfully
get out of bed before 1pm.
The moon the hum of lolos,
balanced by the boisterous
and reserved.

I wave at clouds for my
best friend's father,
a friend's uncles, and
I reassure them everyone
is okay.

I ask the birds to watch over
my cousins and sing for them,
reminders they are loved.

I gossip with my Auntie Linda
and Auntie Marionetta as they
carry leaves from my house to the neighbor,
and they tell me how beautiful I am.

Because I can look at my palms
and behind the petals of years,
tending to a growing
contentedness.

An Ode to (Toxic) Masculinity
for Clarkie

To raised voices and raised fists,

to the collective allowance of
palms to cheek
knuckles to wall

replacing
verbal expression.

To violence,

to their version
of strength that relies on
someone being lesser,
someone being
hurt.

To fear,

where no one questions why
women and others who are vulnerable

are silent as a form of
protection.

To that which will attempt to
prevent my son from being gentle,

soft:

he will
be.

Portrait of Josefa as Lola

I

Longing is the pillow, the two pillows Lola uses for a backrest and butt rest, taking the corner of the couch to watch her nightly movie, sometimes two. Whenever we drive by Auntie's house, she sighs again and criticizes a man who is not here. "Doon," she would point, with her eyes, with her nose, with her lips, with each blink, and I imagine what that must feel like, to witness a wilting, to be enmeshed in an inevitable transition.

Longing is wanting nothing, not looking, the act of pushing away. We kept none of the walkers, nor the canes. I ask if we should at least keep one for her in the future and her eyes burst with smoke, her lips never moving.

II

Patience is the deep sigh Lola makes,
one that erupts from her tsinelas
all the way to her shoulders,
which are less round
and more curled
every year, yet
she still wakes at 7am
to iron her duster
for the following day.

I mistake her patience for being
bagulbol, and we laugh and claim
all of us Masucols are bagulbol.

I ask Lola if she misses her mama,
my Lola Cadia, and before
I can finish the question,
she blurts, yeah,
in a way I know she is
shielding her heart from
an already buried pain,
so I promise not to forget.

Oonga. All of us Cortes-
Masucols are bagulbol.

III.

She sews buttons onto cardigans
and chooses different patterns
to make bandanas for each
of our four dogs and carries
the watering can from the
garage to the backyard,

muttering Cebuano
curse words
to herself,
to the flowers,

but never to us.

My heart
walks out in the world
Abraham A. Joven

III.
HILAK

How will you begin?

I only learned how to cook in 2020. "Real food," others would protest when I bring up my predating sunny-side up eggs covered with tentatively lifted oil and heat against hot dogs, blackened and crisp. Even then, I would add tomatoes and jalapenos, and my lover would praise me because that's what lovers do. I only know where things are placed because I am designated cleaner, housemaid, with a power to return things to normal and dismantle plated towers of pisa in the sink. I have a notebook, in my collections of half-written, unopened notebooks, specifically for cooking. My hoarding an illness only started because my mother read my diary in sixth grade and said I couldn't use "damn" in reference to my cousin thoroughly shutting me up. I refused to write. To talk. To flower. To open. This notebook holds only two recipes. One for kimchi salad and sinigang na liempo, a dish I made three times, before learning my maternal lolo's favorite sinigang *is* sinigang na liempo. But even my signature dish is tempered, adjusted to cater to the taste of the majority. It is everything, anything, it feels, except my own.

November 19, 2020 at 3:50pm

In which I write,
I'm losing patience for Lolo. I can't stand his selfishness and lack of appreciation.

Beneath that,
Pain pills, two every 4-6 hours

my scribbles of two tongues,
clumsily labelled yellow for Tagalog,
orange for Cebuano,

Na antok ko. I wish I could take a nap. Maybe when Lola leaves, I'll take a nap on the couch. It's hard to read with the TV on.

Dahil - because

pressure is a placement of time,
pressure is proof of feeling:

Kabuan - entirety
Pagalok - offer

There is only anger
while I wish from the after:

Sunday	Monday	Tuesday	Wednesday	Thursday	Friday	Saturday
Jamie	Jamie	M		E	Jaden	Jaden

Slept: 12-1:44am,
2-5am,
5-9am

minsan - sometimes
palagi - always

Mabuti palagi siya mag-buhay sa
diary ko.

Asa ang Tanan

1. Where is my sister?
   Is she smiling
   is she breathing?
   Relief found in her laughter with our mother.

2. Where is my mother?
   Is she in pain
   is she okay?
   Gratitude found with her phone in her hand.

3. My father
   reliably at work
   updates via text
   maybe everything
   will be okay.

4. My brother and I: at odds.
   he, craving company,
   I, solace,
   his voice scaling sharply upward
   as he speaks with his friends
   he is home; he is safe.

5. My love. *My love.* My love, my love.
   I shamelessly check his location
   so this is what they mean when your
   heart decides to remove itself from its sleeve

he is apart from me
he is a part of me.

6. My friends text:
    group chats aplenty
    lighting green and blue
    love in bonds take on many forms.

7. The fist in my chest releases. *Snapchat streaks are maintained.*

8. The fist uncurls. *The dogs are fed.*

9. The fist becomes a palm. *Did I take my vitamins? Allergy meds?*

10.   With my books, journal, and pens:
                    I think everything will be okay.

Dalaga

She is nineteen, and he is twenty-two. I am still in her womb. She doesn't know what to do. He is also of her kind, from the same island, forced together as grains of sand are. You all look the same now, don't you? But they're not. He left their home when he was still a boy. He grew up here, accustomed to this land. It still gawked at her, asked her to move to the side, constantly reminded her she took up too much space.

This is not what she wishes for her children, though she is young enough to be considered a child herself. She traded her home for a mindset that revolves around itself: self-concerned, self-obsessed, selfish. Little does she know of the hate that will be spewed back to her because of her eyes or the color of her skin. The mangoes are not the same in this new place. Its shape alien and color wrong. Do they have halo-halo? This swirling dessert makes an example of her life. Though there are blips of brightness over the horizon, there is still darkness we are forced to swallow.

She believes that because I will be born here, acceptance will be inherited. She believes I will never feel meek or undeserving, will never cower. She is wrong, but let her hope. She has much more to worry about.

She will never learn of how this affects me, how the thoughts run through my veins, inserting into my marrow: How can I rebuke her temperament towards me when I am the invader? How can I disparage that which is trying to survive? I who infiltrated without her permission—how she clutched her drenched shirt cursing her luck—how

44

could protest when I cast myself, a pebble into the sea, the recoil reaching its tendrils to each shore? But as the thought lingers, the more comforting it becomes, the more reassuring. She doesn't know yet the burden I will become. For now, I am a safety; I have become a beacon; she is no longer alone.

One day, I will know with each raise of her hand. With each curl of her teeth speaking knives of criticism permeating the flesh, carving each curve into her image. This is what she was able to control, this entity she has the power to alter. She was not the villain. I was. But we are not yet there.

Instead we are when she places a hand atop her belly. It will be okay. She will tell me this story when I am older, when I question the intentions of my origin. She will take a breath. This is the sacrifice, this is what she will give to me, to us, for us to grow. We shall never hunger. We never did hunger. Because of her.

The Effects of Trauma on Impressionable Adolescents
is what it should have read

Dec. 17, 2015,
or was it a few days before?

Legs over heads in a cramped truck
as we said our goodbyes,
embraces between strangers
to fill the crevices in our chest
the nights blurred together
unable to separate point
from blank page.

What was wrong with me?
What allowed skin to wrinkle
into white lines to match the
outside of my eyes
how did the walls
cave unto me?

There were no days back then.

Along with the exchange of hours
poring over self-help and grief
against wet eyes as the pages
cut each finger, forced into grip.

And on the days I was brave,

I would hold suicide and depression
in left and right hands,
hoping that I would always remember

I remember
but now I hate that I do.

**When my future apo ask how their Lolo and I stayed in love during
a pandemic**

We had to, from afar
pink on pink
or pink on brown
we used our imagination
with exhales accented
with giggles,

We had to, from afar
because I sobbed uncontrollably
as he consoled me
through the screen
because we had to remind
each other we are more
than pixels.

We had to, from afar
pillows resemble warmth
and I swear I said it before
but he is always beneath
m(y) e(yes).

Write a List of Your Achievements,
what has lead you to achieve them?

This is for the me that thought they would
be a novelist, a ballerina, an astronaut,
and a doctor all at once,

who would spin in the family room
thinking I could be a sky dancer too.

With my head upside down
legs pushing force up-toward,
scraping different shades of blue

because anything is possible.

Multitudes
for Czaerra Galicinao Ucol

You are leader
with hands to support,
eldest and manghod with
eyes that dare to lock
with arms to exclaim and
fingers to make wit and
laughter with friends who
span miles on opposite ends,
you who is feet planted
in every place you call
home, whose tongue sings
in more than one.

You who is legend,
You who is tender,
You who is only

You.

Personhood

After Alice Notley

I am the straight bark
of the untouched Cebuano palm,
where the lechon is the best
and words fly freely and gahi.

My bones kneaded from
the pearls of my mother's tears,
marking her path from Tondo to Quezon City
to Playa del Rey.

My lips lined with the
kiss between spring and summer,
green and gold, with a laugh
to rival the Pacific.

At night, my hands in prayer
are the grace from the santonilyo
and I ask that my lolo find peace
in the beyond.

And with knees wide enough
to carry the Muntinlupa
eastward slope
into the sunrise,
I smile.

My last name
is a map.
Janice Lobo Sapigao

IV.
KUSGAN

Lineage

On my father's paternal side, there is a legend of our surname's origin. Stemming from the Spanish 'Labrador', a single ancestor, a thief and a rebel, successfully fled Spain.

There are no details spared: we don't know his first name nor his city of origin. We only know his intent: he needed to get away. He shortened his name to avoid capture. My grandfather doesn't know why our ancestor chose the Philippines, or if it were a choice at all. Perhaps the archipelago, this cluster of islands, were simply happenstance.

I am filled with vigor and pride for this lone man; how thrilling it is to be related to a rebel, to have been born from his supposed courage...until my grandfather nonchalantly describes how this same ancestor forced himself upon one of the Filipino natives and she bore him twelve sons and one daughter.

This ancestor would not have known (or perhaps he did, making it worse) the splintered identity, or lack thereof, of the indigenous Filipino people. They did not even refer to themselves as 'Filipino' until the Spanish occupation, as they claimed our land as theirs, dubbing us, 'La Isla Filipinas.'

But, my grandfather tells me this story, so I know to be kind to anyone whose surname shares ours. Also meaning unbreakable in its new country. He tells me this because he laments having six granddaughters from his sons. He voices his languish so blatantly in front of my sister and I.

I often wonder about the thirteenth daughter, where my distant cousins are and how they're faring. I also wonder about the Filipina native, and how I don't know her name.

I don't know how I may honor her.

Acknowledgements

Mohilak is the Cebuano word for "to weep." Cebuano and Tagalog are only two of the 170+ languages in the archipelago of the Philippines.

Translations, in **Cebuano**:

Hilak; to cry.

Luha; tears.

Biyaan; abandon; desert; quit.

Kusgan; mighty; strong.

Pagalok; offer.

Gahi; hard, rough.

Manghod; younger sibling.

Translations, in **Tagalog**:

Anak; child.

Para sa paborito kong tita; for my favorite aunt.

Nakalimutan ko pala; I forgot.

Marias; in reference to the Three Marys. When christened, the daughters of Catholic Filipino parents would have two first names, the first being Maria. Often, a group of girls, whether sisters, cousins, friends, etc., would be referenced as the "Marias." The pronunciation is similar to maría, as found in Spanish. But, Philippine languages don't normally use accent marks outside of language-learning purposes.

Dalaga; a young woman passed puberty not yet married; an

"eligible" young woman.

Apo; grandchildren.

Lolo; grandfather.

Lola; grandmother.

Dahil; because.

Doon; there.

Na antok ko; I'm tired.

Kabuan; entirety.

Minsan; sometimes.

Palagi; always.

Embutido; Philippine meatloaf with ground pork stuffed with hard-boiled eggs, sliced ham, and or various sausages,. Traditionally wrapped in aluminum foil and steamed or baked. Commonly prepared during Christmas, parties, or other special occasions.

Simbang Gabi; Night Mass; a devotional nine-day series of masses in anticipation for Christmas.

Mabuti palagi siya mag-buhay sa diary ko; good thing he'll always be alive in my diary.

Santonilyo; the god of grace prior to Spanish colonization. This god was replaced by the imagery and lore of Santo Niño from Catholic mythology.

Sinigang na liempo; soup with pork. Sinigang means stew, from the Tagalog verb sigang; to stew.

~

"Lineage" was originally published on *Tiny Essays.*

"Dalaga" was originally published with *Ayaskala Magazine.*

"Happy Mother's Day" was originally published in issue 3 of *PHEMME Zine.* The poem was written after Craft Chaps Vol. 1 by Chen Chen following the prompt, 'if you can afford to go to therapy (art can be therapeutic but it's not a substitute for therapy.)

"The Effects of Trauma on Impressionable Adolescents/is what it should have read" was originally published with *Ayaskala Magazine.*

"First" was originally published with *Inqluded Magazine.* This magazine is now defunct.

"The things I didn't know I loved" was written in a workshop facilitated by poet Rachelle Cruz.

A version of "Personhood" was published in the Poems from the 11th Generative Workshop Zine as edited by Sophia Dahlin from May-June 2021.

A majority of these poems were written during the month of April for National Poetry Month in response to generated prompts from *Ayaskala Magazine,* Luya Poetry, and the hashtag #escapril created by multimedia creator and poet, Savannah Brown.

~

December 17, 2015 is a day of heartbreak. I will always see you as a little brother. An Nghi, Larry.

To Jason Bayani and all else involved in the organization of the summer 2021 Interdisciplinary Writer's Lab cohort. To Anthony Cody, Devi S. Laskar, and Trinidad Escobar for being incredible teachers.

To the cohort itself: Vanessa Yee, Dorothy R. Santos, Julian Parayno-Stoll, Joy Ding, Hairol Ma, Nureena Faruqi, Yaminah Abdur-Rahim, Layhannara Tep, Angel Trazo, Tiffany Huang, Jiexi Yuru Zhou, Preeti Kaur Rajpal, Saa'un Bell, and Jessica Kim. Thank you for letting me bask in your brilliance and creativity, all. Wet frogs forever!

To Terry Thunder Tsai, my gentle friend. I hope you find what you're looking for.

To Jennie Asuncion. Thank you for exchanging memes with me. I appreciate you.

For my cousins, or my "practice babies", Orion Phoenix "Pin-Pin", Athena Raine "Baby", Perseus Oliver "Perse," and Artemis Evangeline "Artie." KuRic and I love you all forever and always.

Muchas gracias para mi gemela linda, Ellie Lopez. I'm buying your book next!

So much gratitude to the folks behind The Digital Sala, especially Czaerra Galicinao Ucol, Joseph "Butch" Schwarzkopf, Christian Aldana, Hari Alluri, Rachelle Cruz, and Jason Magabo Perez.

For Manang Janice Lobo Sapigao. Thank you for believing in me. Agyamanak la unay.

To my beloved kumares, Dina Klarisse, Maria Bolaños, and Kelly Ritter, with love. I am inspired by each of you for your passion and drive. I'm where I am because of you three.

To Reginald Imbat, my very best friend. Ayayaten ka!

To sugarcane juice. Lami kaayo ba!

To my pets: Kobe, Pau, Magic, and Sasha. To Mariah and Lucky GreyWolf. I love you.

To the pets in the beyond: Stitch, Fluffy, and Nina. I miss you.

To my parents, my manghod na babae, ug manghod na lalaki.

Always and forever to Eric. Thank you for all the ramen cups and milk teas. Thank you for your eyes and your love. Thank you for holding my hands in yours. Balbaleg ya salamat. Inar-aro taka, love of my life.

Portrait of a Bio as a Poem

Keana Aguila Labra / Key-on-uh / Ah-gi-la / La-bra / they / siya / their /
if you are not / close / the use of she is sacred / she is familial / she is
mare / inday / ate / manang / you cannot use / she / if you are thinking in
/ binaries / Aguila Labra is a 2019 / and 2020 Best of Net nominated /
Cebuana-Tagalog Pilipinx / poet / writer / doodler / crier / who can be
found by pagkain / or with boba / or in a massage chair / mewing at stray
cats / a cannon of laughter / with canons / outside of the mga puti / and
advocate for / Filipinxao / Filo / Filipin@ / Filipinx / any and all
beautiful / identifiers / voices in the / literary / arts residing / on // stolen
// Ohlone Tamien land. / Born and returned / to San José / raised in
Milpitas / where the three way intersection at Curtis Ave / and Comet Dr
/ swells their chest / and she sobs in her car for her purple room / where
the train whistled at 1pm / and 1am / for fifteen years / With roots in /
throughout California / Tracy, Salida, Modesto, / Playa del Rey, / under
the Pacific Ocean / sixteen seventeen eighteen hours / Tondo, Quezon
City, Manila, / Luzon / another flight / dramamine and benadryl aiding
to / Cebu / Ilihan, San Fernando, Mandaue / She is a / staring at the stars
/ INFJ-T / enneagram 2 / neutral good / primary directions / southeast /
year of the wood dog / virgo sun sagittarius moon scorpio rising /
scorpio venus cancer mars libra mercury / in love with personality and
placements / as way of securing a / sense of self / Aguila Labra has
always / *always* being a word of safety / of reliability / of longing / been
passionate / about / poetry / in spiral wired / grey red and blue /
basketball notebooks / confessing to the / moon. / Two books / promoted
Aguila Labra's / affinity / for writing: / Love That Dog by Sharon
Creech / and Locomotion by Jacqueline Woodson. Writing is her outlet
to release any emotion, / whether negative or positive. / As a visual

thinker, / writing allows Aguila Labra / to set time for / herself / set boundaries / make room for / love / and analyze her / thoughts and feelings / her / Self / Although her writings / stem from her / experiences, / Aguila Labra's goal / is to write something that others / may relate to / scream to / weep to / resonate resonate resonate / with / because what is / humanity / if not shared / touches / and lips in way / the space for our skin / can resuture / Writing allows her to overcome her inhibition, / her shyness, / and connect with / others / through writing. / Because quiet / kindness / empathy and compassion / are always strengths / They / (a reminder / to always alternate / her / them / a reminder to always associate / nonbinary / genderflux / genderfae / demigirl / pangender / to Aguila Labra) hope to / foster / a creative safe space / for Pilipino / Filipino / Pinoy-Pinay-Pinxy / and all ethnolinguistic groups / and all Indigenous Peoples / sa Pilipinas / and underresourced, / and underrepresented / communities / uplifting as we climb // always // with their online magazine, / *Marías at Sampaguitas.* / Outside of *Marías,* they're a columnist / for *Headcanon Magazine* / and aims to join *The Walang Hiya Collective* / They write reviews / scattered thoughts thoughts thoughts / of literature and / media / anime / comics / komiks / handmade and otherwise / through a / feminist womanist / inclusive / lens on their Medium @Cebuana / and (attempt at a) Bookstagram and Mangastagram / account at @Tambokekai. / which is in the same vein as the Tagalog / Buchichay / or Butchokoy / They / taught / and want to teach more / Q&A poetry workshop(s) / with *Teen Belle Magazine* / with NCPASA / and hope to host / virtual book club sessions / (they're on the app, Bookclubz! / join us! / add them!) / in the / near / future. / Their micro-chapbook / their anak / *Natalie* / was published / with *Nightingale & Sparrow,* / and their chapbook, / anak / *No Saints,* / with *Lazy Adventurer Publishing.* / And their chapbook *Mohilak* with *Fahmidan Publishing & Co.* / respectively / gemini, scorpio, & libra anak / Their mini-chapbook *(I am) Still* / was briefly published with *Violet & the Bird,* a / now / defunct press. / now transformed with a new name / *(I am) Still* is now / *Kanunay* / who is / forthcoming / a new anak / late 2021. / Daghang salamat sa imong pasensya ug / gugma.